AF726585

How to Get $1M in Credit and Keep It

Secrets of Long-Term Credit Growth and Control

By Joe Correa

Published by Live Stronger Faster

Copyright © 2025 by Joe Correa

All rights reserved.

No part of this publication may be reproduced, distributed, or transmitted in any form or by any means—electronic, mechanical, photocopying, recording, or otherwise—without the prior written permission of the publisher, except in the case of brief quotations embodied in critical reviews and certain other noncommercial uses permitted by copyright law.

This book is for educational and informational purposes only. The author and publisher are not engaged in rendering legal, financial, or other professional advice. Readers should consult a qualified professional before making any financial decisions.

First Edition

Table of Contents

Introduction 5

Chapter 1: Understanding the $1M Credit Blueprint 8

Chapter 2: The Personal Credit Foundation – Your First Million Starts Here 19

Chapter 3: Building Business Credit Without a Personal Guarantee 30

Chapter 4: Credit Stacking — How to Build Credit Fast Without Getting Shut Down 41

Chapter 5: Keeping the Credit — How to Protect, Grow, and Never Lose What You Built 52

Chapter 6: Using Credit to Build Income, Not Just Buy Things 62

Chapter 7: Building Business Credit That Doesn't Rely on Your Personal Credit 72

Chapter 8: How to Work with Banks and Lenders to Unlock Bigger Limits and Better Terms 82

Chapter 9: Automate, Monitor, and Review — How to Maintain a Million in Credit with Less Stress 93

Chapter 10: From Credit to Capital — How to Turn Limits Into Leverage, and Leverage Into Legacy 103

Final Words from the Author: "Credit Is Just the Beginning" 113

Epilogue: "From Credit to Legacy — What Comes After the $1M Milestone" 118

Introduction

Building a Million in Credit Isn't a Dream — It's a Strategy

When most people hear "$1 million in credit," they picture private jets, luxury cars, and high-risk lifestyles. But the truth is, building seven figures in credit isn't about showing off—it's about unlocking control. Control over your finances. Control over your business. Control over your future.

In this audiobook, you'll learn the step-by-step blueprint for how I—and thousands of others—built well over a million in total available credit. Not just personal credit, but business credit too. You'll learn how to get it, how to manage it, how to avoid common traps, and most importantly, how to keep it working for you long-term.

This isn't just theory. You'll get real examples, real numbers, and practical steps that you can follow whether you're just getting started or already have strong credit and want to go to the next level.

Why This Book Matters Now More Than Ever

Banks are tightening. Lenders are cautious. And AI is starting to make credit decisions faster and more data-driven than ever. That's both an opportunity and a threat. If you understand how the system works, you can use it to scale—responsibly and sustainably. If you don't, one bad move can cost you everything you've built.

This book is about longevity and leverage. You'll learn how to position yourself to:

- Get $100,000 in new credit every 3–6 months
- Maintain lender trust and avoid shutdowns
- Turn credit into income-producing assets
- Build business credit that doesn't rely on your personal guarantee
- Monitor and protect your credit profile like a pro

Whether you're a real estate investor, business owner, or entrepreneur looking to scale, this audiobook will give you the full roadmap to hit the $1M mark—and stay there.

The Structure of This Audiobook

Each chapter is designed to be easy to follow, starting with a step-by-step instructional format followed by a real-world story that shows the lessons in action. At the end, you'll find a complete checklist and strategy summary to help you implement what you've learned.

If you've made it to Book 9 of this series, you're already ahead of 99% of the population. Let's keep going. Let's break the barrier. And let's do it smart.

Welcome to **"How to Get $1M in Credit and Keep It."** Let's begin.

Chapter 1: Understanding the $1M Credit Blueprint

What Does $1M in Credit Actually Mean?

Before we begin chasing numbers, let's define them. Getting to $1 million in credit doesn't mean holding a million in debt. It means having access to credit—secured or unsecured—that adds up to a seven-figure total.

This includes:

- Personal credit cards with high limits
- Business credit cards and lines of credit
- Personal and business loans
- Revolving credit lines like HELOCs
- Equipment and vendor financing

The key difference between amateurs and experts is **control**. Professionals build access to large credit limits without maxing them out. They use credit strategically, not emotionally.

- ❖ **Rule #1:** Getting $1M in credit is not a one-time event—it's a layered strategy of approvals, management, and growth over time.

The Four Pillars of Million-Dollar Credit

To reach this level, you need to build on these four pillars:

1. **Strong Personal Credit Foundation**
   - 720+ FICO score
   - At least 3–5 primary accounts over 3+ years
   - Low credit utilization (<10%)
   - No recent derogatory marks
2. **Established Business Credit Profile**
   - Active LLC or Corporation
   - D-U-N-S Number with strong Paydex score
   - Vendor trade lines reporting to business credit bureaus
   - Separate EIN and business bank account
3. **Strategic Credit Applications**
   - Applying for cards and credit in batches (credit stacking)

- Targeting lenders that pull from different credit bureaus
- Leveraging 0% intro APR and balance transfer offers to fuel growth

4. **Responsible Credit Behavior**
   - Never carry high balances on personal cards
   - Pay early or on time, every time
   - Keep a strong mix of credit (revolving and installment)

Building in Phases – From $0 to $1M

Most people fail because they try to jump from $10K in credit to $1M in one leap. Here's a phased approach that works:

Phase 1: The First $100K

- Personal cards from high-limit lenders (Amex, Chase, Navy Federal)
- Business credit cards from your existing bank (e.g., Capital One Spark, Chase Ink)
- 2–3 vendor tradelines reporting to D&B and Experian Business

Phase 2: The $250K Tier

- Add LOCs (Lines of Credit) and credit union cards
- Apply for business fuel cards, fleet cards, and store credit
- Establish 6+ tradelines and 3+ personal cards with low balances

Phase 3: The $500K+ Leap

- Leverage relationship banking for large LOCs and term loans
- Request credit limit increases every 6 months
- Use personal credit as a guarantor if needed to secure initial large lines

Phase 4: The $1M Positioning

- Access 5–7 business credit cards with limits above $30K
- Use high-limit personal cards as a foundation for asset purchases
- Add strategic financing tools: equipment financing, invoice factoring, HELOCs on investment properties

The Hidden Traps That Kill Long-Term Credit

It's not just about getting the credit. It's about keeping it. These traps destroy long-term access:

1. **Over-utilization** – Carrying high balances will trigger lender concern, even if you're paying on time.
2. **Inactivity** – Accounts can be closed for inactivity, especially business cards.
3. **Hard pull stacking without strategy** – Applying randomly can get you blacklisted.
4. **Mixing personal and business expenses** – Especially on business cards—this raises red flags.
5. **Cross-default clauses** – Missing one payment on a bank product can cause other accounts to be closed.
6. **Unreported changes** – Change in income, business structure, or address can invalidate your terms.

Your 90-Day Action Plan to Start

Let's set some real-world goals you can accomplish in the next 90 days:

Week 1–2

- Check your personal credit report from all 3 bureaus
- Open a business bank account
- Get your D-U-N-S Number (free from Dun & Bradstreet)

Week 3–4

- Apply for 2–3 net 30 vendor accounts
- Apply for a business credit card (e.g., Chase Ink or Amex Blue Business)
- Ask for a credit limit increase on one personal card

Month 2

- Make on-time payments to vendor accounts
- Use less than 10% of your personal credit limit
- Open a credit union account and explore LOC options

Month 3

- Apply for 1–2 more business cards with different banks
- Begin tracking your business Paydex and Experian Business score

- Schedule your next round of credit limit increases

❖ **Pro Tip:** Stay consistent. Credit growth is exponential, but only if you master the fundamentals.

The Wake-Up Call

Michael Reynolds sat in his small home office in Tampa, Florida, sipping his coffee while staring at his laptop screen. The same spreadsheet he'd looked at for weeks taunted him: $42,000 in total available credit, maxed-out cards, and a business idea going nowhere fast.

He had good intentions. Two years ago, he started a mobile detailing business, funded by a single personal credit card. No business account. No LLC. Just hustle.

Now, he was burned out, behind on payments, and terrified that one more late fee would tank his credit score. He'd never even heard of business credit—until one YouTube video changed everything.

In that video, the speaker said something Michael couldn't forget: **"You can get $1 million in credit if you follow the process—but only if you treat credit like a business asset, not a lifeline."**

Something clicked.

That night, Michael stayed up until 2 a.m. Googling terms like "business tradelines," "DUNS number," and "credit stacking." By the time he closed his laptop, he had a new goal: rebuild his credit the right way and build $1 million in total credit across personal and business lines.

Rebuilding the Foundation

Michael started with the basics.

He pulled all three of his personal credit reports, identified the high utilization that was killing his score, and called each creditor to negotiate better terms. He applied for a secured card with a credit union and committed to paying it off weekly.

Next, he formed **Reynolds Auto Solutions LLC** and opened a business bank account with Navy Federal. It was a simple step—but it changed everything. Suddenly, he was being treated like a business, not just a broke guy with a side hustle.

He applied for a **D-U-N-S number**, ordered a virtual office address, and signed up with Uline and Grainger—two vendor accounts that reported to Dun & Bradstreet. Within 30 days, those accounts showed up on his business credit profile.

When he checked his Paydex score 60 days later, it was 80.

"Now I can build," he thought.

The Credit Stacking Strategy

With his personal credit utilization down to 9% and three business tradelines reporting positively, Michael moved into what he called "Phase 2"—strategic applications.

He learned to group his credit applications in **batches**, targeting lenders that pulled from different bureaus. He applied for a **Chase Ink Preferred** (approved for $15,000), an **Amex Blue Business Plus** (approved for $20,000), and a **Capital One Spark Cash** (approved for $10,000).

In just 30 days, his total credit jumped from $42,000 to **$87,000**.

Three months later, he repeated the process. He requested credit limit increases, opened new business lines with Sam's Club and Shell Fleet, and kept usage low.

When he hit $150K, it finally sank in—he was playing a different game now.

But the real test was coming.

Temptation and Discipline

Success was intoxicating. With over $200K in available credit,

Michael got offers for everything—loans, credit cards, even luxury car financing. He almost said yes to a Tesla Model Y he didn't need.

But he remembered the rule: **"Just because you have credit, doesn't mean you use it recklessly."**

Instead, he invested $50K into building an online detailing course, set up an ad campaign, and hired a VA to help run the business backend. Within 6 months, the course brought in $6,000/month in passive income.

With that income, he was never late on payments. He kept utilization under 7%, paid off his balances weekly, and requested increases every 6 months like clockwork.

By year two, he had six business cards, five vendor tradelines, two business LOCs, and four personal cards—totaling **$1.1 million in available credit**.

Legacy Over Leverage

Now 37, Michael mentors other entrepreneurs. He teaches them that million-dollar credit isn't about racking up debt. It's about leverage, discipline, and building long-term trust with banks and institutions.

He tells his students:

> "If you chase credit like cash, it'll ruin you. But if you build credit as a tool—strategically, intentionally—you'll have more power than most people ever imagine."

Michael didn't become a millionaire overnight. But with a solid plan, disciplined execution, and long-term thinking, he earned what most people only dream about: control, freedom, and legacy.

And it all started with a late night, a spreadsheet, and a decision to take credit seriously.

Chapter 2: The Personal Credit Foundation – Your First Million Starts Here

Why Personal Credit Is Still King

Even if your end goal is to build massive business credit, your personal credit score will always play a key role—especially in the early stages. Lenders use your personal FICO score to gauge your overall risk. A weak personal score can disqualify you from high-limit cards, lower your business credit approvals, and block you from crucial funding opportunities.

To put it simply: **If your personal credit isn't solid, your $1M credit strategy will crumble.**

Here's why personal credit matters:

- It's often required to **personally guarantee** business credit cards or loans
- It reflects your **financial habits** to lenders and partners
- It's the foundation for **mortgages, car loans, and HELOCs**

- It can **fast-track approvals** when applying for large lines of credit

If you're starting below 700, this chapter is your game plan to get to 740+ and stay there.

Anatomy of a High FICO Score

FICO scores range from 300 to 850, and you need to be at **720 or higher** to access the best rates and limits. Here's how your score is calculated:

FICO Score Breakdown:

1. **35% – Payment History:** Late payments are credit killers. Even one can drop your score by 50+ points.

2. **30% – Credit Utilization:** Try to stay below 10% of your total credit limit across all cards. Below 30% is okay, but <10% is optimal.

3. **15% – Length of Credit History:** The longer your accounts are open, the better. Don't close old accounts unless absolutely necessary.

4. **10% – New Credit Inquiries:** Limit hard inquiries to 2–3 every six months. Too many can trigger denials or lower scores.

5. **10% – Credit Mix:** A healthy mix includes revolving credit (credit cards) and installment loans (car loans, student loans, etc.).

- ❖ **Action Step:** Pull your credit report from all 3 bureaus (Experian, TransUnion, Equifax) and dispute any inaccurate items.

Repair, Rebuild, and Optimize

Whether your score is 650 or 800, there are always ways to improve or optimize it for strategic growth.

If Your Score Is Below 700:

- **Dispute inaccuracies** on your credit report using tools like Credit Karma or Experian Boost.
- Apply for **secured credit cards** or credit-builder loans.
- Ask family or friends with good history to **add you as an authorized user** on their cards.
- Pay off collections and negotiate for **"pay-for-delete"** arrangements when possible.

If Your Score Is 700–750:

- Keep utilization low and begin requesting **credit limit increases** every 6 months.
- Open a **new high-limit card** from a top-tier bank (e.g., Amex, Chase).
- Maintain perfect payment history.

If Your Score Is 750+:

- Use your strong credit to **apply for large business credit lines** with a PG (personal guarantee).
- Begin leveraging your credit to fund **income-producing assets** (real estate, digital products, etc.).

❖ Pro Tip: Keep your total personal card balances below $1,000—even if you have $50K in available credit. It's not about how much you're allowed to spend, it's how little you actually use.

Credit Habits of Million-Dollar Borrowers

Building a strong credit foundation isn't just about what you do once—it's about the habits you build and repeat every month. High-limit borrowers and wealth builders tend to follow these rules:

❖ Golden Credit Habits:

- **Pay in full** before the statement date (not just due date)
- **Avoid carrying balances** into the next month unless using a 0% promo offer
- **Check scores monthly** using free services or paid monitoring
- **Never co-sign** for others—it's a shortcut to disaster
- **Use autopay** to prevent accidental missed payments
- **Negotiate annual fees or request waivers** on premium cards
- **Track due dates and utilization** with apps like Credit Karma, Mint, or MyFICO

If you want to keep $1M in credit, you have to look like someone the banks can trust with $10M. That means discipline, transparency, and precision.

Build Personal Credit with These Tools

Now that you understand the habits and structure, here are powerful tools and resources to help speed up your credit journey:

❖ Tools That Work:

- **Experian Boost** – Instantly adds on-time utility and phone payments to your Experian report
- **Self (formerly Self Lender)** – Credit-builder loan that adds installment credit history
- **Navy Federal Credit Union** – High-limit cards for members with strong internal scores
- **Amex EveryDay Preferred** – Good for long-term usage and limit growth
- **Capital One Venture X** – Premium card with business applications and strong limit growth potential

30-Day Checklist:

1. Pull all 3 credit reports and fix errors
2. Set up autopay for every card or loan
3. Keep balances <10% (ideally 1–3%)
4. Request 1–2 credit limit increases

5. Apply for 1 strong personal card if ready

❖ Warning: Do NOT apply for multiple cards unless you've checked which bureaus they pull from. Spread applications to avoid excessive hard pulls on one report.

Next Step: Now that your personal credit foundation is solid, it's time to build **business credit without a personal guarantee** — that's the topic for Chapter 3.

The Credit Denial That Changed Everything

Ava Morales stood in line at her local bank, nervous but excited. After three years of running her mobile notary business in Orlando, she was finally applying for a small business line of credit. She had built a loyal client base, maintained decent income, and wanted to scale.

But when the banker returned, he didn't have good news.

"I'm sorry, Ava. You were denied. Your FICO score is a 612, and there are some red flags."

Her stomach dropped. She'd paid her bills—mostly. But she'd made the classic mistakes: maxed out two cards during a slow season, paid one credit card 32 days late, and ignored a $58 medical bill that went to collections.

She felt humiliated—but determined.

That night, she made a decision: she was going to fix her personal credit no matter what. And not just fix it—she was going to build a bulletproof score so no lender could deny her again.

The Repair Begins

Ava spent the weekend researching everything she could on credit repair. She signed up for **Credit Karma** and ordered her **three full credit reports**.

She found:

- One late payment (Capital One, 32 days late)
- A $58 collection (a lab bill she never received)
- Two cards maxed out: $3,000 limit with a $2,950 balance, and a $1,500 card at $1,400

She didn't panic. She made a plan.

First, she **called the collection agency**, paid the $58 in full, and got them to agree to a "pay-for-delete." Next, she called Capital One, explained the late payment, and politely asked if they'd remove the late mark as a courtesy. They said no—but she added a consumer statement explaining the one-time issue.

Then she **cut her spending by 40%**, used her side income to pay down the high balances, and set up **autopay on every single account**.

By the end of Month 1, her score jumped to **662**.

Rebuilding Strategically

In Month 2, Ava opened a **Self credit-builder loan** and added herself as an **authorized user** on her cousin's long-standing Amex card with a $10,000 limit and perfect payment history.

That one move gave her an instant credit age boost, raised her available credit, and pushed her score to **693**.

Excited, she reached out to **Navy Federal Credit Union** and opened an account. Because she had a military spouse, she qualified for membership. She applied for their **CashRewards card**—and was approved for **$5,000**.

It was the first time she had a card approved over $2,000. It felt like a turning point.

Her mindset shifted. She started treating her credit like a business asset, not a reactive tool. She paid off every card

before the statement date, used no more than 3% of her limit, and checked her score weekly.

By Month 5, her FICO score hit **737**.

Unlocking Real Leverage

With her credit now in the 700s, Ava finally felt ready to try again.

She applied for:

- **Amex Blue Cash Preferred** (approved: $8,000)
- **Discover It** (approved: $6,500)
- **Capital One Quicksilver** (approved: $7,000)

Instead of celebrating by spending, she focused on preserving the gains. She rotated small recurring bills across her cards—Spotify, her phone bill, and monthly software. Everything else went through her business account.

By Month 8, she'd built:

- A 790 FICO score
- $28,500 in total personal credit limits
- Zero late payments

- Zero balances carried forward

She was now in a position to apply for **$25K–$50K business cards** with a personal guarantee—and she was ready.

A Whole New Game

Ava walked back into that same bank 10 months later. This time, she brought her new business tax ID, proof of income, and her pristine credit report.

She wasn't just applying for a loan—she was **positioning her business** for growth.

The banker reviewed her file, nodded, and smiled.

"You've really turned things around. We can offer you a $40,000 business line to start, backed by your personal credit."

Ava grinned. This was just the beginning.

From 612 to 790, from denied to approved, from reactive to strategic—Ava had proven that anyone with the right mindset, the right tools, and enough discipline could build a foundation strong enough to hold **$1 million in credit**.

Her motto became simple: **"Credit is power. But only when you control it."**

Chapter 3: Building Business Credit Without a Personal Guarantee

Why Business Credit is the Fast Lane to $1M

While personal credit is the foundation, **business credit is the acceleration**. It allows you to access funding that doesn't report to your personal credit report, avoids damaging your debt-to-income ratio, and—most importantly—**can grow much faster** than personal credit.

And here's the key: you can build business credit **without using your Social Security Number or a personal guarantee (PG).**

This is what separates high-level credit users from everyone else. Business credit is reported to commercial bureaus like:

- **Dun & Bradstreet**
- **Experian Business**
- **Equifax Business**

Your goal is to build a strong business profile that lenders trust—so they approve large limits without tying it to your personal credit.

Setting Up Your Business for Credit Success

Before you apply for a single business card or vendor account, your business must be "credit ready." Lenders look at several factors to determine if your company looks legitimate and fundable.

Fundable Business Checklist:

- **LLC or Corporation** – Sole proprietors are high-risk. Form an LLC or Inc. through your state's website.
- **EIN from IRS** – Free from the IRS website. Do not use your SSN.
- **Business Bank Account** – Open this right after forming your business. All expenses must run through this.
- **D-U-N-S Number** – Register for free at Dun & Bradstreet. This is your business credit identity.
- **Business Phone Number** – Get a dedicated number (e.g., Grasshopper or Google Voice).
- **Professional Email & Website** – Use a domain-branded email (e.g., info@YourCompany.com) and basic website.

- **Business Address** – Use a virtual business address if you work from home (e.g., Regus, Opus, or iPostal1).

❖ Warning: Mismatched addresses, phone numbers, or inconsistent business info across credit apps will trigger red flags.

The Tier System of Business Credit

Think of business credit like climbing stairs. You can't jump to the top tier overnight. You build your profile by progressing through **credit tiers**, each one unlocking more powerful funding opportunities.

Tier 1: Net-30 Vendor Accounts

These accounts give you supplies or services on credit and report to business bureaus. Start with:

- **Uline** (office supplies)
- **Grainger** (tools and industrial supplies)
- **Quill** (cleaning and office items)
- **Summa Office Supplies**
- **Nav.com** (business credit monitoring)

Buy something small, pay within 30 days, and repeat for 3–6

months. These tradelines will begin reporting.

Tier 2: Store Cards (PG Optional)

Once 3–5 tradelines are reporting, apply for store credit cards like:

- **Amazon Business**
- **Sam's Club**
- **Office Depot**
- **Staples Business Advantage**

Some may ask for a personal guarantee, but others don't if your business credit file is strong.

Tier 3: Fleet Cards

Used for fuel and auto maintenance:

- **WEX Fleet**
- **Shell Business**
- **Fuelman**

These are often no-PG with a strong business profile.

Tier 4: Business Credit Cards & LOCs

With 6–8 tradelines, solid payment history, and revenue proof, you can qualify for:

- **Amex Blue Business Cash**
- **Chase Ink Business Unlimited**
- **Divvy or Brex** (modern no-PG fintech cards)

Keep It Separate and Clean

Many entrepreneurs ruin their business credit by **mixing it with personal spending** or by skipping essential business practices.

Rules for Using Business Credit Responsibly:

- **Never use personal credit for business expenses** (especially if trying to get non-PG cards)
- **Keep business purchases consistent and necessary** (supplies, software, marketing—not personal vacations)
- **Pay off business accounts early**—even earlier than net terms
- **Track all purchases and categories** in your bookkeeping software (e.g., QuickBooks or Wave)

Also, make sure to **monitor your business credit reports** regularly. Errors are common, and they can destroy your credibility without notice.

- ❖ Pro Tip: Sign up for **Nav.com** or **CreditSignal** by Dun & Bradstreet to track your Paydex and Experian Business scores for free.

90-Day Business Credit Building Blueprint

Month 1: Foundation

- Form LLC and apply for EIN
- Get business phone, email, and address
- Open a business checking account
- Register with Dun & Bradstreet and get your D-U-N-S number

Month 2: Tradelines

- Open 3–4 Net-30 accounts (Uline, Quill, Summa)
- Make small purchases and pay invoices in full before due date
- Monitor for when tradelines start reporting

Month 3: Growth

- Apply for 1–2 Tier 2 store cards (Amazon Business, Office Depot)
- Request business credit limit increases if available
- Apply for a business monitoring service to track your Paydex and Experian Business score

Once these steps are complete, you'll be positioned to apply for your **first $10K–$50K in real business credit**—without ever tying it to your personal credit score.

- ❖ Remember: This process takes consistency. Business credit grows faster than personal credit—but only if you respect the structure.

Darren's Business Credit Playbook

Rock Bottom and a New Beginning

Darren Price had been a high school economics teacher for over a decade. He loved teaching but hated the paycheck. Every year, inflation crept up, and his salary barely moved. He dreamed of starting a financial literacy company for teens—but he had one major problem.

His credit score was okay. Not amazing—just okay. But more

importantly, he didn't want to risk his personal credit or co-sign anything. With a family of four, he wasn't willing to bet their future on a business that hadn't proven itself yet.

So instead of applying for loans or personal credit cards to fund his dream, Darren went down a different path: **business credit without a personal guarantee.**

He didn't know anyone else who'd done it. But after months of reading, watching, and obsessing over credit-building strategies, he decided: if this is real, I'm going to make it work.

Making His Business "Lender Ready"

The first thing Darren did was legitimize his business.

He created **SmartStart Youth, LLC**, applied for an **EIN**, and opened a **business checking account** with a local credit union. He made sure the business had:

- A virtual address (not his home)
- A dedicated business phone line
- A branded domain email (info@smartstartyouth.com)
- A basic website outlining his services

He then registered for a **D-U-N-S number** on Dun &

Bradstreet and created a free account on **Nav.com** to monitor his business credit activity.

No one had ever taught him this in his finance degree. But within two weeks, he had what looked—on paper—like a 10-year-old company.

The First Credit Moves

Darren started by ordering $40 worth of printer paper and markers from **Uline**. He paid the invoice five days early.

Then he ordered light cleaning supplies from **Quill**, followed by office accessories from **Grainger**. He repeated the same process: buy small, pay early, let it report.

He made sure **nothing was purchased personally**. Every order was logged in a spreadsheet and paid through the business account.

After three months, he saw it: three tradelines were reporting to Dun & Bradstreet and Experian Business. His Paydex score was 80.

It felt like a win.

By Month 4, he applied for his first non-PG store credit card—**Office Depot Business**. He was approved for $2,500.

Then came **Amazon Business**, **Staples Advantage**, and **Shell Fleet**. Approvals started coming more easily, and his confidence grew.

> "I was finally building something that didn't depend on my personal name," he later said. "It was like watching a separate version of myself grow financially."

Growth Without Guarantees

At Month 6, Darren's small curriculum packs were selling on TeachersPayTeachers and Shopify. Revenue was modest—$1,000/month—but his business profile was strong.

That's when he decided to apply for his first big leap: the **Divvy Business Card**—a modern fintech card that didn't require a PG.

Approved. $6,000 limit.

Then came **Brex**, followed by an offer from a local bank for a $15,000 line of credit—all approved based solely on his business performance and tradeline strength.

He was now at **$42,500 in business credit**, with **zero ties to his personal credit report**.

His personal score never dropped. No hard pulls. No risk to his family's finances. And every single account was paid in full, early, and tracked meticulously.

Darren's Business Credit Philosophy

Today, Darren speaks at school board conferences and parent associations across the Southeast. His company, SmartStart Youth, is now making over **$8,000/month**, and his business credit limit sits at **$126,000**—with more applications in the pipeline.

His advice to new entrepreneurs is simple:

> "Don't think of credit as a backup plan. Think of it as a growth engine. And never, ever confuse your personal credit with your business ambitions."

He continues to use vendor accounts, Tier 2 cards, and business-only loans to fund expansions—still without any personal guarantees.

From teacher salary to six-figure business credit, Darren proved that building wealth through credit doesn't require risk—it just requires **structure, patience, and professionalism.**

His personal goal? "$1 million in business credit. No shortcuts. No personal guarantees. Just smart, disciplined growth."

Chapter 4: Credit Stacking – How to Build Credit Fast Without Getting Shut Down

What Is Credit Stacking?

Credit stacking is the strategy of applying for multiple high-limit credit cards or lines of credit **in a short window of time** across different lenders, **without triggering red flags** or damaging your score. The goal is to maximize approvals before the new accounts or inquiries show up on your reports.

Used correctly, this strategy can unlock $50K–$250K in new credit within 90 days. Used recklessly, it can get you flagged, denied, or blacklisted.

Why It Works:

- Most lenders only see **their own inquiry in real time**
- There's a **24–72 hour lag** before new applications or approvals hit the credit bureaus
- Strategic planning allows you to take advantage of this lag and build fast, without panic

- ❖ Key Principle: You're not "gaming" the system—you're simply **understanding timing, bureau pulls, and risk management.**

Timing and the 48-Hour Rule

The biggest risk in credit stacking is spreading out your applications. If you apply for Card A today and Card B next week, B may see A's new inquiry—and deny you.

To avoid that, apply within a **tight 24–48 hour window**, using this sequence:

1. Personal credit cards first (if needed)
2. Business credit cards next
3. Lines of credit and high-limit business funding last

Why this order? Because business cards often don't show up on personal credit, and LOCs are more conservative with approvals.

- ❖ Pro Tip: Use tools like **CreditBoards.com** or **Doctor of Credit** to find out which bureaus each lender pulls from, and plan accordingly.

Bureau Diversification – The Smart Stacking Advantage

Not all lenders pull from the same credit bureaus. This is a key element of smart stacking.

Example Breakdown:

- **Chase**: Typically pulls **Experian**
- **Amex**: Often pulls **Experian**
- **Navy Federal**: Usually pulls **TransUnion**
- **Capital One**: Pulls from **all 3 bureaus**
- **Discover**: Often pulls **Equifax**

By choosing lenders that pull from **different bureaus**, you can:

- Avoid multiple hard pulls on the same report
- Protect your score from sudden drops
- Spread inquiries evenly across your profile

This allows you to stack 3–6 approvals with minimal impact on any single bureau.

How to Prepare for a Stacking Round

Pre-Stack Checklist:

- Credit score above 720 (ideally 740+)
- Utilization under 10% (ideally under 5%)
- No new inquiries in the past 60 days
- Business is credit-ready with 3+ tradelines reporting
- All recent payments made early or on time

Application Flow:

1. Day 1 AM: Apply for 2 personal cards (e.g., Amex Platinum, Chase Sapphire)
2. Day 1 PM: Apply for 2 business cards (e.g., Amex Blue Business, Chase Ink)
3. Day 2 AM: Apply for 1–2 more business cards or LOCs (Divvy, Brex, regional banks)

Keep a spreadsheet to track:

- Application date
- Lender and product
- Approved/denied status
- Credit bureau pulled

- Credit limit received

❖ Tip: Request **credit limit increases** on your existing cards 2 weeks prior to stacking. This boosts your total available credit and score.

After the Stack – Protecting Your Profile

The stacking round is done—but your work isn't.

Here's how to protect your new approvals and ensure long-term growth:

Post-Stack Action Plan:

- **Freeze new applications** for 3–6 months to avoid suspicion
- **Keep utilization under 10%** on each card and under 5% total
- Set **autopay for all new accounts**
- Call lenders to request **monthly reporting**
- After 90 days, **request credit limit increases** on all new cards

Avoid applying for more credit too soon. Lenders monitor new accounts and will shut down cards if they see excessive growth that looks risky.

- Red Flag Behaviors:
    - Applying for 10+ cards in 2 weeks
    - Maxing out newly opened cards
    - Missing first payments or making only minimums
    - Shuffling balances aggressively between cards

Used correctly, credit stacking can help you leap from $25K to $150K in credit **without harming your score**. Used carelessly, it can destroy your credibility overnight.

Stack smart. Stack small. Stack intentionally.

Naomi's 3-Day Credit Leap

A Bold Goal with No Room for Error

Naomi Carter was no stranger to hard work. She'd built her online nutrition coaching business from scratch, working nights and weekends while raising two kids as a single mom in

Atlanta. But now, her business was ready to scale—and she needed funding.

Her plan? Launch a digital course series, run ads, and hire a VA. The challenge? She didn't want outside investors or personal loans. She wanted to use credit—but **do it without compromising her score or triggering red flags.**

So she turned to something she'd heard in an obscure podcast: **credit stacking**.

The host claimed he got over $100K in new credit in 3 days. Naomi was skeptical—but intrigued. If this worked, it could change everything.

Prepping for the Stack

Naomi wasn't going in blind.

She spent two weeks preparing her personal and business credit:

- Her **FICO score** was 752
- Credit utilization was down to **3%**
- She had **3 tradelines reporting** to D&B
- Her LLC, website, and EIN were set up properly

- She reviewed her reports on **Credit Karma** and **Nav.com**

Next, she mapped out which lenders pulled from which bureaus:

- **Amex** – Experian
- **Chase** – Experian
- **Navy Federal** – TransUnion
- **Capital One** – All 3
- **Discover** – Equifax

She created a spreadsheet. Her goal: **apply to six cards in 48 hours across three bureaus**, to avoid stacking hard inquiries on one.

The clock was ticking.

The 48-Hour Execution

Day 1, 8:00 AM Naomi applied for the **Amex Business Gold**. She got instant approval for **$20,000**.

Day 1, 9:30 AM Next was **Chase Ink Unlimited**. Approved for **$15,000**.

Day 1, 12:00 PM She submitted her **Capital One Spark Business** application. This one wasn't instant—it went to manual review. She moved on.

Day 1, 3:00 PM She hit submit on the **Navy Federal Business Rewards card**. Approved—**$12,000** limit.

Day 2, 9:00 AM She applied for **Divvy**. Instant approval for **$10,000**.

Day 2, 11:00 AM Final card: **Brex**, based on business performance. She linked her business account, showed consistent revenue, and got approved for **$8,000**.

By 5:00 PM, the Capital One manual review came back—approved, **$10,000** limit.

In just two days, Naomi secured **$75,000 in business credit**—and none of it appeared on her personal credit report.

She didn't just beat the system. She used it the way it was designed to work—if you understood it.

Strategic Use, Not Flashy Moves

Temptation hit quickly. Naomi got ads in the mail for business equipment leasing, travel cards, and startup loans. She ignored them.

Instead, she:

- Spent $2,500 on course design and production
- Paid a graphic designer and VA through her business Amex
- Used Divvy to run Facebook and YouTube ads
- Left the other cards untouched for now

Her goal wasn't to spend all the credit. It was to **build trust** with each lender by using small amounts and paying them back early.

She added every card to her project tracker. Due dates, statement dates, utilization goals—all mapped out.

Her score didn't drop. Her business didn't stall. And within 60 days, she was generating **$6,500/month in new revenue**.

Naomi's Rules for Credit Stacking

Naomi now teaches other women how to build and fund online businesses through smart credit use. Her core rules:

> "If you're stacking credit to spend, you'll fail. If you're stacking credit to build systems, you'll win."

She tells her students:

- Stack across bureaus, not in one place
- Don't apply for too many cards in one day—spread it over 48 hours
- Only stack when you're fully prepared—no rushed decisions
- Track everything like a CFO, not a shopper
- Don't brag about how much credit you have—prove it by how you use it

Within 6 months, Naomi's business had crossed **$100K in annual revenue**, and she had access to over **$110,000 in credit**—without hurting her personal credit at all.

And it all started with a spreadsheet, a deadline, and a strategy most people never learn.

Chapter 5: Keeping the Credit — How to Protect, Grow, and Never Lose What You Built

The Reality of Losing Credit Overnight

Getting to $1M in credit is impressive—but keeping it long-term is where true mastery lies. Many people build large credit lines only to **lose them within a year** due to poor management, risky behavior, or lender crackdowns.

- ❖ A single misstep—like a late payment, sharp credit score drop, or sudden cash advance—can trigger **automatic limit reductions or account closures**.

So while earlier chapters taught you how to build and stack credit, this chapter is about how to **protect** it, **grow it safely**, and **ensure it works for you long-term.**

Red Flags That Get Accounts Shut Down

Banks and lenders don't always give you a warning. They monitor your behavior behind the scenes using risk algorithms, AI tools, and internal scoring.

Here are the biggest credit-killing behaviors:

1. High Utilization Across Cards

Even if you pay on time, using 80–90% of your credit line consistently is a red flag. It signals financial distress.

2. Late Payments

Just one 30-day late payment can drop your score 50–100 points and lead to automatic closures.

3. Opening Too Many Accounts Too Fast

If you continue applying aggressively after a stacking round, it looks like desperation and raises risk scores.

4. Cash Advances

Lenders see cash advances as a signal that you're short on funds. Avoid them unless absolutely necessary.

5. Mixing Personal and Business Funds

Using your business card for personal purchases can violate terms of service and result in a sudden closure.

- ❖ Pro Tip: Set up **alerts** for due dates, keep utilization below 10%, and monitor your reports monthly.

Strategies to Keep and Grow Your Credit

Keeping your credit is about routine, discipline, and communication. Here's how high-limit users protect and expand their credit long-term:

1. Request Credit Limit Increases (CLIs) Every 6 Months

Many lenders allow "soft pull" increases online. Increasing limits boosts your total available credit and lowers your utilization ratio.

2. Use All Cards Lightly

Don't let any account go unused for more than 6 months. Lenders close inactive accounts.

3. Build Relationships with Bankers

Local or regional banks still rely on relationships. Get to know your banker. Ask what they need to extend new credit.

4. Schedule Recurring Payments

Use small recurring charges (like subscriptions) on each card to maintain activity and payment history.

5. Create a Credit Calendar

Track statement dates, reporting dates, and due dates for all accounts. This prevents payment overlap and late reporting.

Monitoring Tools and Automation

As your credit empire grows, manual tracking becomes inefficient. Smart credit users rely on tools to stay ahead.

Recommended Tools:

- **Nav.com**: Monitors both business and personal credit
- **Experian Business**: Tracks business credit score changes
- **Credit Karma & MyFICO**: For alerts on personal credit activity
- **Tiller or YNAB**: Budgeting tools that sync with accounts
- **Google Calendar**: For payment reminders and statement tracking

You can even use tools like **Plaid** or **Zapier** to automate data collection for business reporting.

❖ Review your full credit report every 90 days. Catch errors, unexpected inquiries, or any signs of identity fraud early.

Future-Proofing Your Credit

If your goal is $1M+ in credit, you'll eventually attract attention from underwriters, fraud prevention teams, and relationship managers. Here's how to future-proof yourself:

Smart Habits:

- **Keep business and personal finances completely separate**
- **Avoid any sign of financial instability**—large cash advances, missed payments, or over-leveraging
- **Diversify across institutions**—don't let one bank control too much of your credit
- **Build assets, not liabilities**—use credit to buy income-generating tools, not luxury items
- **Reassess every 90 days**—what can you increase, renegotiate, or shift?

Legal and Strategic Considerations:

- Use **LLCs and holding companies** to manage risk and separate ventures
- Consult with a CPA to ensure you're reporting correctly

for tax and credit purposes

- Consider forming a relationship with a **business banker or advisor** once your credit exceeds $500K

The end game isn't just access to credit—it's using credit to build **real, lasting wealth.**

How Jordan Almost Lost Everything

Jordan Lyles had done the impossible. At just 29 years old, he'd built over **$200,000 in personal and business credit** in less than a year. A former retail manager turned e-commerce entrepreneur, Jordan had leveraged credit stacking, built a sleek Shopify store selling sustainable pet products, and landed a viral moment on TikTok.

Sales hit $20,000 in a single week. He celebrated with a trip to Tulum, upgraded his laptop, and booked a branding coach.

For the first time in his life, **he felt like he'd made it.**

But three months later, he logged into his Capital One dashboard and froze.

> "Credit limit reduced from $15,000 to $3,000."

Then Amex followed suit. Then Chase. One by one, the limits dropped—without warning.

His business hadn't failed. His products still sold. So what happened?

Missteps That Cost Him Dearly

When Jordan retraced his steps, the red flags became obvious:

1. He'd used **80–90%** of his Amex limit to pay for product inventory.
2. He made **two minimum payments** during a slower sales month.
3. He pulled **cash advances** from his Chase card to cover emergency shipping fees.
4. His new ads hadn't performed, leading to a negative cash cycle.
5. He'd opened **four new business cards** right after a stacking round—within 30 days.

To him, it felt like smart scaling. To lenders, it looked like he was panicking. His behavior triggered **automated risk alerts** across multiple accounts.

They didn't care about his TikTok success. They cared about **risk**—and his profile suddenly screamed it.

Damage Control and Humility

Jordan spent the next month in triage mode. He paused all ad spend. Canceled unnecessary subscriptions. Paid down $15,000 in balances using reserve funds he hadn't touched in months.

Then he did something most people never consider: **He picked up the phone.**

He called every bank and asked to speak to an account manager—not to complain, but to take responsibility.

He told them:

> "I scaled too fast, didn't manage my limits properly, and I understand the reduction. I'm taking steps to stabilize and would like to rebuild our relationship."

Some were cold. A few were kind. Most thanked him for calling—something they rarely heard.

One banker even said:

> "We usually only hear from people after they've defaulted. You're ahead of the curve."

Learning to Protect the Castle

Jordan turned the experience into a lesson in **credit protection**.

He created a "Credit Castle" board in his office with five pillars:

1. **Utilization Below 10%** at all times
2. **No Cash Advances — Ever**
3. **Limit Increases Every 6 Months**
4. **No New Applications Within 90 Days of a Stack**
5. **Separate Funds for Emergencies**—credit is for scaling, not survival

He set **alerts for every card's due date**, used **Nav.com** to track his business credit, and reviewed all reports monthly.

Three months later, Amex restored his original limit. Then Chase did. Then Capital One.

The lesson was clear: building credit was only part of the journey—**maintaining it was the mission**.

Legacy Over Leverage

A year after the scare, Jordan's Shopify business had grown past $500K in revenue. He now had over **$300,000 in total credit**, but only used about 4% monthly—and paid it off weekly.

He had four bank relationships, two business credit lines, and a rock-solid personal score of 786.

When asked by a podcast host what he'd tell entrepreneurs chasing high credit limits, Jordan didn't talk about cards or points.

He said:

> "Protect it like your home. Don't spend credit like cash. Respect it like capital. If you don't, the banks will remind you who's really in charge."

Jordan had come dangerously close to losing everything—but emerged wiser.

Now, every new credit approval came with a sticky note he kept above his desk:

"Getting credit is temporary. Keeping it is forever."

Chapter 6: Using Credit to Build Income, Not Just Buy Things

The Most Dangerous Misuse of Credit

Once you've secured access to tens or even hundreds of thousands of dollars in credit, one of two things will happen:

- You use it to **buy income-producing assets**, or
- You use it to **buy things that lose value** and trap you in debt

Most people choose the second. They buy vacations, luxury items, or non-essential upgrades under the illusion that having credit equals having cash.

But million-dollar credit users don't think that way. They know:

- **"Credit is capital. Capital should create income, not expenses."**

In this chapter, we shift from building credit to **leveraging credit**—without getting burned. You'll learn how to use credit as a **tool to create cash flow**, so your payments are always covered and your wealth grows while your risk shrinks.

What Makes an Asset vs. a Liability?

It starts with redefining what credit should fund. Ask one simple question:

Does this purchase bring money in every month—or take money out?

Credit-Worthy Income-Producing Assets:

- **Digital Products**: Online courses, ebooks, templates
- **Rental Real Estate**: Airbnbs, long-term units, multifamily properties
- **Audiobooks & KDP Publishing**: Scalable intellectual property
- **Automated E-commerce**: Dropshipping or branded products with proven demand
- **Marketing for Proven Offers**: Running paid ads with high conversion
- **Licensing & Software Tools**: For businesses that use tech to scale revenue

Risky or Non-Recoverable Purchases:

- Cars or equipment that doesn't earn

- Inventory without market research
- Personal items bought on business cards
- Vacations, weddings, gifts
- Paid ads with no validated product or offer

Rule: Use credit to buy **scalable cash flow**, not consumable satisfaction.

Core Credit-Funded Business Models

Let's walk through **three proven business models** where people routinely use credit to build scalable income.

1. Digital Product Business

- Cost to create: $500–$3,000
- Funded by: Business cards, 0% APR offers
- ROI potential: $1K–$15K/month Use credit to create and market ebooks, courses, templates, or bundles. You build once, earn forever.

2. Real Estate Investment

- Cost to enter: $10K–$100K (down payment, rehab)

- Funded by: Personal/business cards, HELOCs, LOCs
- ROI: $500–$5,000/month per property Use business credit or HELOC to fund down payments or renovations on short-term rentals, then refinance or rent for profit.

3. Ad-Funded Online Sales

- Cost to launch: $2K–$10K (ads + inventory)
- Funded by: Business cards, fintech lines
- ROI: $2K–$20K+/month Use cards to launch paid ads on proven product funnels. Track ROAS (Return on Ad Spend) and scale only if profitable.

❖ Remember: Always have a repayment plan before you charge your card. Credit is only leverage when used responsibly.

Pay-Down Strategies That Keep You Safe

Using credit for business growth only works if you **manage your repayment strategy.** Here's how to structure your cash flow.

Strategy 1: The Float Method

Use 0% APR credit cards to fund a product or campaign. Repay before the intro period ends (usually 12–18 months).

Strategy 2: Weekly Auto-Pay from Revenue

Set your Stripe, PayPal, or other revenue processors to auto-transfer weekly to pay off cards.

Strategy 3: Rolling Profits into Payments

Split every dollar earned:

- 50% to credit repayment
- 30% to reinvest in marketing
- 20% to personal savings

This structure allows you to **grow your business without growing your debt.**

Also, track **credit card billing cycles** and pay strategically **before the statement date**, not just the due date, to keep reported balances low.

Final Tips for Using Credit to Create Wealth

Start with a Small Win

Use $1,000–$2,000 in credit to create a micro-product or a small ad campaign. Build confidence before scaling.

Stack Capital, Not Purchases

Use your access to build repeatable income, not just cover expenses.

Separate Growth & Maintenance Accounts

Have one card for recurring business expenses and another for scaling projects. This prevents overuse on a single account.

Track ROI Like a CFO

Use tools like Google Sheets, QuickBooks, or YNAB to know exactly how much every dollar of credit earns—or loses—you.

Never Bet the House

Never use personal credit to fund risky experiments without validation or proof of concept.

- ❖ Your mindset shift: "Credit isn't money to spend—it's a weapon to multiply results."

Lina's Digital Empire

The First Swipe That Changed Everything

Lina Morales had always dreamed of building something of her own. Working as a paralegal by day and raising two kids at night left little time—but plenty of motivation.

She wasn't trying to get rich quick. She just wanted to create income that didn't rely on 40-hour weeks. That's when she came across a YouTube video on digital products. The idea of making money from ebooks, templates, and downloadable planners sounded too good to be true—until she realized people were doing it every day.

There was only one problem: she had **no savings**.

But she did have a **$4,000 business credit card** with a 0% APR for 12 months.

After weeks of hesitation, she swiped it. $1,700 went to a course on digital marketing and Canva design. Another $800 went to hiring a Fiverr freelancer for her product mockups and logo.

With just $1,500 left on her card and zero room for mistakes, Lina pressed "Publish" on her first Etsy shop.

First Sales, First Panic

For two weeks, nothing happened. No clicks. No sales. She second-guessed everything.

Then came the first sale. A $7.99 downloadable wedding planner. Then another. Then a $27 bundle pack. Within 30 days, she had made $412—small, but real.

Encouraged, she reinvested $400 from her next paycheck into Etsy ads and expanded her product line. This time she stayed lean—designing everything herself.

By Month 2, her total credit usage was down to $800. Sales for the month hit $2,300. She began to understand something she'd never been taught:

> "If I use credit to build something that pays me back monthly, I never have to go into real debt."

Scaling Smart

Lina kept her expenses disciplined. She never touched the card for groceries or bills—only for tools that moved the business forward.

She used $300 to buy a course on SEO and $200 on upgraded listing photography. Slowly, she improved her store's visibility. By Month 3, she was profiting $1,100/month after ad costs.

She started paying off her card **weekly**, sometimes even **daily**, using the float strategy.

A few months later, she launched a second store with niche digital content for teachers. She funded the launch with another business card—this time from Chase, approved for $12,000.

She used only $1,500 of it and built that store to $3,000/month in revenue by Month 6.

She didn't just grow a business. She learned to use credit as **a tool for expansion, not consumption.**

Risk, Reinvestment, and Control

Lina knew she couldn't stay small forever. She wanted to hit $10,000/month, but not by working 16-hour days. So she hired a virtual assistant using credit, trained her over Zoom, and handed off order processing and customer service.

Then, she invested in **Facebook and Pinterest ads**—but slowly. She tested $5–$10/day using her Amex Blue Business card. Her rule was simple: if an ad didn't return at least 2X within 5 days, she cut it.

Her business never owed more than $3,000 across $30K+ in credit. Her **utilization stayed under 10%**, and her business Paydex score rose to 85.

She paid off her original $4,000 card in full by Month 8.

That same week, she crossed **$6,200 in monthly profit** across her two stores—and hadn't dipped into personal savings once.

The New Rulebook

Lina's friends were stunned. "Wait... you built all that on credit?"

She laughed, then explained: "No, I used credit. But I built it with discipline."

Her new rules were printed and taped above her desk:

1. **Credit only for cash-flow-producing expenses**
2. **Track ROI on every dollar spent**
3. **Never spend before a plan to repay**
4. **No emotional purchases on business cards**
5. **Scale what's working, pause what's not**

Today, Lina makes over **$100,000 a year in digital profit**, works from home, and has access to over **$75,000 in credit** across multiple business cards—with no debt.

Her final insight?

> "I didn't need funding. I needed a framework. Credit gave me the chance to build one—and income gave me the freedom to pay it off."

She turned plastic into profit—and made her dream of financial freedom real.

Chapter 7: Building Business Credit That Doesn't Rely on Your Personal Credit

The Power of True Business Credit

Most entrepreneurs never separate their personal and business finances—and it holds them back.

They max out personal cards to cover business expenses. They co-sign for every loan. They absorb all the risk. But smart credit users know: the real wealth is built when your **business stands on its own.**

❖ The ultimate goal: **No PG (Personal Guarantee)** required. That's when you know your business is truly fundable.

In this chapter, you'll learn how to:

- Build and grow credit under your business's EIN—not your SSN
- Qualify for lines and cards without risking your personal credit
- Create a credit profile that banks trust—even without years of history

Understanding No-PG Business Credit

What is No-PG Credit? It's a credit line, card, or loan issued to your business that's **not personally guaranteed by you.** This means:

- Your personal credit isn't pulled
- The debt won't show up on your credit report
- You're not personally liable if the business defaults (though default still hurts)

But No-PG isn't given out freely. Lenders want to see:

- A strong business credit file (Paydex score, Experian Business, Equifax Biz)
- Consistent revenue
- Industry stability
- Positive payment history from vendors or previous business accounts

How to Build a No-PG-Eligible Business Profile

Here's how to position your business to qualify:

Step 1: Business Legitimacy

- LLC or Corporation (not a sole prop)
- EIN from the IRS
- Business bank account with monthly activity
- Business phone number, website, and branded email
- Virtual or commercial business address

Step 2: Business Credit Profile

- Register for a **D-U-N-S Number** (free at DNB.com)
- Open 3–5 Net-30 vendor accounts that report (Uline, Quill, Summa Office)
- Pay vendors early to boost your Paydex score
- Monitor your business credit monthly via **Nav.com** or **CreditSignal**

Step 3: Add Tier 2 and Tier 3 Accounts

After 90 days of tradeline history:

- Apply for **store credit cards** (Amazon, Sam's Club, Office Depot)
- Apply for **fleet cards** (WEX, Shell, Fuelman)

- Use them lightly, pay in full

Step 4: Apply for No-PG Credit Cards

Once your business credit is established:

- Apply with fintech platforms like **Brex**, **Ramp**, or **Divvy**
- Explore banks like **Truist, Regions**, or local credit unions with no-PG business offers
- Avoid applying for cards that require your SSN unless necessary

Keys to Keeping Your No-PG Status

Even if you secure No-PG credit, lenders can revoke or change terms based on risk.

To protect it:

- Maintain **on-time payments** across all tradelines
- Keep balances low (under 30% utilization)
- Continue building your business credit file
- Avoid using personal cards for business
- Build revenue and cash flow that matches your credit

usage

❖ Pro Tip: Never mix personal and business expenses—keep accounting, cards, and transactions fully separate to avoid legal and financial risk.

Tools and Platforms for No-PG Expansion

Here are some tools and platforms to fast-track your business's No-PG credit access:

Credit Monitoring

- **Nav.com** – Shows real-time Paydex, Experian Biz, and Equifax Biz scores
- **CreditSafe** – Business credit data reports for B2B lenders
- **Dun & Bradstreet CreditSignal** – Alerts you to changes in your D&B file

No-PG Lenders and Platforms

- **Brex** – Based on business revenue, not credit
- **Divvy** – Budget-based platform with real-time tracking
- **Ramp** – For funded or high-cash-flow businesses

- **Torro Funding**, **BlueVine**, **Fundbox** – For revenue-based lending

- Local banks and credit unions that issue corporate cards

❖ Final Word: When your business qualifies on its own, you're no longer dependent on your personal credit—and that's when the real freedom begins.

Daniel Journey to True Business Credit

Tired of the Risk

Daniel James had built a name for himself in the custom furniture space. What started in his garage grew into a profitable Shopify store with steady Instagram traffic and local word-of-mouth. But despite the growth, something kept bothering him:

> "Every loan I took. Every credit card I used. Every financing agreement—I was the one personally responsible."

He'd personally guaranteed over $80,000 in business debt. When the economy shifted and orders slowed, his personal credit score dropped, even though the business still had cash flow.

That was Daniel's wake-up call. If he was going to turn his company into a sustainable legacy, it couldn't be built **on his back alone.**

He needed **business credit that stood on its own.** No more using his Social. No more risking his personal credit every time he scaled.

Starting the No-PG Game

Daniel got serious about his company's structure.

He upgraded from a DBA to Daniel **James Designs, LLC.** He opened a new business bank account and applied for an **EIN**. He bought a virtual office address downtown and set up a business line through RingCentral.

He registered for his **D-U-N-S Number**, then opened accounts with **Uline, Quill, and Summa Office Supplies.**

Instead of large orders, he bought $50 to $100 in supplies—sandpaper, gloves, even paper towels—and paid early.

By Month 3, he had five tradelines reporting to Dun & Bradstreet. His **Paydex score hit 80.**

> "That was the first time a lender saw my business without asking for my personal credit," he said.

Doors Open Without a Signature

With his foundation in place, Daniel started applying for **No-PG credit options.**

First up: **Divvy.** Approved for $8,000.

Next: **Brex.** Approved for $12,000 based on revenue from Shopify and Square.

He applied for an **Amazon Business Card** through his LLC—no PG. Approved for $4,000.

He added a **Shell Fleet Card**, a **Sam's Club Business Card**, and even got a $5,000 **WEX Fleet** line to help with delivery vehicle expenses.

In less than 6 months, Daniel had secured **over $40,000 in business credit—without putting his Social Security number on a single application.**

He could finally breathe.

> "It was like building a wall between me and risk," he explained. "The business could grow—and I could sleep at night."

Smart Use and New Leverage

Daniel didn't go on a spending spree. He used his No-PG credit strategically.

- **Divvy** paid for ad testing
- **Amazon** stocked packaging materials
- **Brex** covered new website design
- **Fleet cards** fueled his delivery vans
- All payments were made **before** the statement date

His utilization never went above 20%. His business credit profile stayed clean. And most importantly, **his personal credit score went up**—because he wasn't over-leveraged anymore.

Soon, a banker from his credit union called him.

> "We noticed your business is growing. You may qualify for a $50K business LOC—no PG, since we've seen consistent deposits for 9 months."

He applied. Approved.

Legacy Without Liability

Today, Daniel has over **$120,000 in business credit**, all tied to his EIN—not his SSN.

He tells every new business owner he mentors the same thing:

> "If your business can't stand on its own credit legs, you're not building a business—you're just borrowing with a fancy name."

Daniel now uses credit to fund expansion, bring in contract workers, and finance inventory that earns him profit within 30–60 days. He hasn't needed a personal guarantee in over a year.

His dream of creating a sustainable, scalable brand is now rooted in smart financial architecture—not personal sacrifice.

And when his son asked him recently what it means to "own a business," Daniel replied:

> "It means I take the risk with a plan—and protect our future while I build it."

Chapter 8: How to Work with Banks and Lenders to Unlock Bigger Limits and Better Terms

Stop Hiding From Banks—Start Building Relationships

Most people avoid banks unless they need something. But the smartest credit users know that building relationships with banks is the **key to unlocking higher limits, better rates, and flexible approvals.**

- Relationship banking can unlock **$50K–$250K+** in credit and funding—even when automated systems say no.

The further you go in your credit journey, the more human relationships matter. Underwriters review large credit decisions. Commercial bankers recommend clients for loans. And business development reps often pre-qualify clients for exclusive offers.

If you want high-limit credit that grows with you, don't just build your credit profile—**build your lender profile** too.

Understanding the Bank's Perspective

Banks don't just lend money—they manage risk. To them,

you're not just a score; you're a data profile made up of:

- Account activity and deposit history
- Average daily balances
- Business cash flow trends
- Past repayment behavior
- Account tenure and relationship strength

That's why people with "average" credit scores sometimes get approved for huge lines—because they've built trust with the bank over time.

- ❖ Relationship lending isn't about asking for money—it's about showing you're worth betting on.

Banks offer three levels of value:

1. **Consumer banking** – Personal accounts and cards
2. **Small business banking** – Business checking, business credit cards, merchant services
3. **Commercial banking** – High-level lines, equipment loans, real estate funding

As your credit access grows, you'll move through these tiers—and the relationships you build in each one matter.

How to Become a Bank's Ideal Client

Here's how to make banks want to lend to you:

1. Maintain High Average Balances

Even if it's short-term, keeping $5K–$10K in your business account shows you're managing cash wisely.

2. Make Frequent Deposits

Banks love activity. Weekly or biweekly deposits—even small ones—show consistent revenue.

3. Use Their Products

Use their merchant services, credit cards, or savings accounts. This strengthens your profile internally.

4. Ask About "Soft Pull" Pre-Approvals

Many banks offer pre-qualification that doesn't hurt your credit. This can fast-track access to large limits.

5. Get a Dedicated Business Banker

Having a single point of contact increases your chances of getting offers others never hear about.

- ❖ Example: Local and regional banks often offer $25K–$100K business lines of credit with low documentation—**if you already bank with them.**

Preparing for a Big Credit or Loan Ask

When you're ready to request a credit line increase or apply for a major business loan, come prepared:

The Lending Toolkit:

- Last 3–6 months of business bank statements
- Profit & loss statement (simple format using Wave or QuickBooks)
- Copy of your business license and EIN letter
- Personal credit report (only if PG is required)
- Business credit report (Paydex or Experian Biz)

Frame the conversation like this:

> "I'm planning to expand X and need flexible access to funding. Based on my account history, what would you recommend?"

Don't ask for a specific number. Let them guide you.

Also ask:

- What credit bureau do you pull from?
- Do you report to business credit bureaus?
- Can this be issued without a personal guarantee?

Long-Term Credit Growth Through Bank Relationships

The wealthiest credit users don't apply endlessly online—they build deep ties with 2–3 institutions.

Here's what that looks like over time:

Year 1–2:

- Open a business checking account
- Apply for an entry-level business credit card
- Maintain strong deposits and clean credit history

Year 3–4:

- Ask for larger lines of credit (LOCs or term loans)
- Leverage commercial banking offers for real estate or equipment
- Get assigned a relationship manager

Year 5+:

- Negotiate custom lending terms
- Qualify for private lending packages
- Access investment-grade funding backed by assets

❖ Final Tip: Relationships don't replace good credit—but they **multiply its value.**

When you're on a first-name basis with your banker and they know your growth plans, they stop seeing you as a number—and start seeing you as a partner.

How Camille Built a $250K Credit Relationship

The Door No One Told Her About

Camille Foster had always avoided banks. Not because she was irresponsible—just cautious. As the founder of a small but growing event planning business, she kept her money in a basic online checking account and used a few credit cards she'd found through blogs and forums.

She never missed payments. She had a 752 personal score. And yet, when she applied for a business line of credit online, she was denied.

> "Too little banking history."

That phrase haunted her. She realized she had strong credit—but no **relationship** with a lender who could actually fund her next level.

Camille didn't need to borrow $5,000. She needed access to **$50,000–$100,000** to expand her inventory, hire help, and say "yes" to the bigger, more lucrative events she kept turning down.

So she walked into her local credit union for the first time in years—and began what would become a game-changing journey.

The First Meeting That Changed Everything

Camille didn't know what to ask, so she kept it simple:

> "Hi. I run a growing event business and I'm looking to build a stronger relationship with a local bank. What kinds of business services do you offer?"

That question opened the floodgates.

Within 30 minutes, she had:

- A business checking account
- A meeting scheduled with a small business advisor
- A brochure of services she'd never even heard of: merchant services, SBA microloans, equipment financing, and internal pre-approvals

The business advisor, Karen, told her:

> "Honestly, people wait until they need money before they come to us. But it's smarter to start the relationship before the ask."

Camille made a promise to herself: she would show up—not just for the loan—but for the long-term.

Deposits, Discipline, and Data

Camille began depositing every client payment directly into her new business account—even the small ones. She automated transfers, maintained an average monthly balance over $5,000, and set alerts to track every transaction.

Karen checked in monthly. "Keep doing what you're doing," she said. "We're noticing."

Three months later, Camille applied for a business credit card. Approved: $15,000 limit.

She used it to pay vendors and suppliers, always paid it off before the statement closed, and kept usage under 10%.

After six months, she asked:

> "I'd like to explore a business line of credit for upcoming contracts. What do you recommend based on my account activity?"

This time, the answer wasn't no.

It was:

> "You're eligible for up to $50,000. No personal guarantee required."

From Denied to Pre-Approved

With her credit union line in place, Camille stopped applying for random online funding offers. Instead, she focused on growing deeper with two more institutions: a regional bank and a fintech lender her advisor recommended.

She repeated the process:

- Opened accounts
- Made consistent deposits
- Used their products wisely
- Asked about **soft pull pre-approvals**

Within 18 months, Camille had:

- $15K credit card at her credit union
- $50K line of credit (no PG)
- $35K equipment loan for event décor
- $100K revolving business line with her regional bank
- $50K Brex line for marketing and automation tools

Total credit: **$250,000**—all from **3 institutions**, built through relationships and smart behavior.

Teaching the Next Generation

Now earning over $30K/month in her business, Camille trains new event professionals in her city on how to scale responsibly.

She always includes one overlooked module in her curriculum: **How to build banking relationships.**

Her advice is simple:

> "Don't just open accounts. Introduce yourself. Ask how to grow. Treat your banker like your CFO."

She explains how relationships helped her secure funding, unlock better terms, and protect her business when a big client backed out of a $60K contract.

Because she had a history of trust, her lender extended a temporary working capital line—**within 48 hours.**

Her final piece of wisdom?

> "Your credit opens the door. But your reputation with a lender keeps it open—and sometimes, makes it automatic."

Chapter 9: Automate, Monitor, and Review — How to Maintain a Million in Credit with Less Stress

The Hidden Threat — Neglect

Most people assume the biggest risk to their credit is misusing it. In reality, the biggest threat is **neglect.**

- Forgetting due dates
- Ignoring changes in your credit profile
- Letting business tradelines go inactive
- Missing subtle signs of fraud or account errors

❖ Your credit doesn't collapse from one big mistake—it erodes slowly when you stop paying attention.

That's why top-tier credit users automate 80% of their management. This chapter is about building a **credit maintenance system** so you don't have to manually track everything while still protecting—and growing—your million-dollar access.

Set It and Forget It – Smart Automation Strategies

Autopay for All Cards

- Set **autopay to minimum** on all credit cards to avoid missed payments
- Then, manually pay full statement balances **before** the due date
- This double layer ensures you never miss a due date—even if distracted

Scheduled Weekly or Biweekly Payments

For revolving accounts (especially high-limit cards), set recurring payments from your business account every Friday or biweekly to lower utilization throughout the month.

Expense Rules

Use tools like **Divvy, Ramp, or QuickBooks** to categorize and limit employee spending on business cards.

❖ Bonus: These tools also sync with your accounting software and flag overspending in real-time.

Credit Monitoring – Stay Alert, Stay Safe

Monitoring your credit is non-negotiable if you have over

$100K in open credit.

Monitor Your Personal Credit:

- **MyFICO.com** – Real FICO score updates from all 3 bureaus
- **Experian Premium** – Offers alerts, score simulations, and identity protection
- **Credit Karma** – Free and good for soft monitoring, especially TransUnion/Equifax

Monitor Your Business Credit:

- **Nav.com** – Shows your Paydex score, Experian Biz, and Equifax Biz in one place
- **Dun & Bradstreet CreditSignal** – Free alerts when changes happen
- **CreditSafe** – Detailed risk scoring used by lenders

Set **monthly reminders** to check your reports—even if everything is automated.

❖ Remember: Catching a single error, data breach, or misreport can save you thousands.

Monthly and Quarterly Reviews

Even if most of your system is automated, you should do **a short review every month** and a **deep review every 90 days**.

Monthly Review Checklist:

- Check balances and due dates
- Look for unexpected charges or account changes
- Ensure no utilization spikes
- Request credit limit increases if eligible
- Confirm new tradelines are reporting

Quarterly Review Checklist:

- Pull personal credit reports from all 3 bureaus
- Pull business credit reports (Nav or D&B)
- Evaluate which cards or accounts are inactive
- Consider consolidating or replacing underperforming cards
- Update your strategy based on new revenue, expenses, or goals

- Pro Tip: Set Google Calendar events or use apps like Notion or Trello to create a recurring credit review workflow.

Protecting the Fortress You Built

Once you've built a seven-figure credit structure, your mindset must shift from **builder to protector**.

Ongoing Credit Habits:

- Never co-sign or let others use your credit
- Use 5–10% of each account monthly to keep it active
- Avoid large spikes in spending unless you have the cash on hand
- Keep cards diversified across issuers (Amex, Chase, FNBO, regional banks, etc.)
- Freeze inactive cards you don't want closed, and store card info securely

Also consider:

- **Setting up credit freeze/security alerts** with bureaus
- **Using a business VPN and password manager**

- Keeping a hard copy of key credit data in a secure location

❖ Your goal: Turn credit into a quiet, stable engine in the background—not a loud fire to constantly manage.

How One Mistake Almost Cost Elijah His Empire

A Silent Misstep

Elijah Benton was a systems guy. His tech consulting business had scaled to six figures in under 18 months, and he had built over **$220,000 in business and personal credit.**

He used credit like a pro—stacked it, leveraged it for growth, and maintained a solid 790+ score.

But there was one thing he hadn't set up: **a system for maintenance.**

One month, while traveling to speak at a fintech conference, Elijah missed a single payment on a $6,000 Amex card. Not because he didn't have the money—because he forgot.

The result?

- A 30-day late mark

- A drop from 792 to 718
- A sudden closure of two smaller cards
- A denied request for a $100K business line he'd been pre-approved for

"It took 3 minutes to make the mistake," he said later, "and six months to rebuild the trust."

Cleaning Up the Mess

When Elijah returned, he did a full audit of his financial activity. What he found was shocking:

- Five cards hadn't been used in 3+ months
- Three due dates were within the same 2-day window
- Two vendor tradelines had stopped reporting due to inactivity

His system had worked—**when he had time to manage it.** But now that his business was growing, he realized he needed **automation and monitoring** that didn't rely on memory or spreadsheets.

He created what he now calls the "Credit Command Center."

Automating Everything

Step one was **autopay on every account**, with a backup alert for any payment over $500.

He separated his cards into categories:

- **Growth cards**: used for ad spend, marketing, and scaling
- **Maintenance cards**: used for recurring bills like software and subscriptions
- **Storage cards**: used once a quarter to keep them active

He used **Notion** to build a simple dashboard with due dates, statement dates, and credit limits. He linked it to his **Google Calendar** and set up:

- Weekly reviews on Fridays
- Monthly full balance checks
- Quarterly credit report pulls from all 3 bureaus

He signed up for **Nav.com**, **Experian Premium**, and **Dun & Bradstreet CreditSignal**.

Now, he got alerts for:

- Any change to his score

- Any new inquiry or account
- Any vendor that stopped reporting

System = Sanity

Within 90 days of setting up his system:

- His personal credit bounced back to 760
- He got re-approved for his $100K business line
- He requested and received **credit limit increases** on 4 of his cards
- He spotted a duplicate charge on a vendor account and resolved it before it hit his credit

His stress dropped. His confidence returned. And his team began using the system too—especially his VA, who could now manage credit activity without needing to guess or ask every time.

> "I went from credit being a checklist item to it being a controlled, living part of my business."

Teaching Others to Protect the Empire

Today, Elijah mentors other entrepreneurs who've built strong credit but struggle with **maintenance**.

He teaches one core belief:

> "If you treat credit like a project, it'll always fall apart. But if you treat it like a system, it'll protect you forever."

His "Credit Command Center" system is now used by over 300 of his consulting clients—and every one of them starts by answering the same question:

"If you stopped managing your credit for 30 days, would it survive or collapse?"

Elijah's story proves that having access to credit isn't enough. Protecting it with automation, structure, and monthly awareness is what keeps your million-dollar foundation intact.

Because at the highest level, **credit isn't about hustle—it's about systems.**

Chapter 10: From Credit to Capital — How to Turn Limits Into Leverage, and Leverage Into Legacy

Credit is the Starting Line, Not the Finish

Most people believe that getting access to large amounts of credit is the end goal. But in reality, that's just the beginning.

- **Credit is not wealth. Credit is leverage. Wealth is built when you use that leverage to create scalable, protected, and income-generating assets.**

In this final chapter, we shift focus from credit-building to **legacy creation**—using your credit profile to launch businesses, fund investments, and build a financial structure that serves your family and your future.

The same $100K in credit that destroys one person's life can generate lifelong income for someone with the right mindset and tools.

Leverage Defined

What is leverage? It's using borrowed money (in this case, credit) to earn a return that exceeds the cost of that money.

Good leverage grows your income and asset base without overstretching your risk. Bad leverage creates liabilities that collapse when the economy shifts or revenue dips.

Smart Credit Leverage:

- Funding digital products that earn passively
- Running profitable ad campaigns for services or e-commerce
- Investing in rental properties and using short-term credit to rehab
- Building businesses that can be sold (digital agencies, SaaS, etc.)

Risky or Toxic Leverage:

- Buying luxury items with no income attached
- Relying on debt to survive instead of grow
- Running expenses across personal cards with no business infrastructure
- Using cash advances to fund loss-heavy ideas

Rule: Only leverage when the outcome is **predictable, profitable, and protected.**

Protect the Downside, Multiply the Upside

If you're going to use $50K or $500K in credit, you need a **plan for both profit and protection**.

Protect the Downside:

- Keep 3–6 months of operating cash in reserve
- Never max out more than 40% of total available credit
- Diversify funding sources (use 4–6 different institutions)
- Always use business structures (LLC, S-Corp) to limit liability
- Insure physical and digital assets

Multiply the Upside:

- Build recurring revenue streams (subscriptions, rental income, memberships)
- Use credit to buy time: hire VAs, automate systems, free up your schedule
- Use your credit profile to qualify for **real estate, SBA loans, or acquisitions**

Strategy: Use credit to fund systems, not just sales. Systems scale. Hustle burns out.

Creating Long-Term Financial Independence

True wealth isn't just about having money—it's about building **financial infrastructure** that works without your daily effort.

Use Credit to Fund These Legacy Moves:

- **Buy properties** that can be passed to your kids
- **Create content-based businesses** that sell 24/7 (courses, audiobooks, publishing)
- **Fund a family trust or holding company** that separates wealth from personal risk
- **Start a credit repair, tax, or funding agency** to help others while generating cash flow

You can also use business credit to:

- Pay for **estate planning**
- Fund **retirement accounts through your LLC**
- Invest in your children's education or first businesses

Credit is temporary—but what you build with it can last for generations.

Exit Plan and Wealth Transfer

You didn't build your credit empire just to coast. You built it to exit smarter, freer, and more secure than when you started.

❖ Final Moves:

- Get your business or portfolio **valued**—know what it's worth
- Use credit to polish, market, or expand before selling
- Sell digital or physical assets for a lump sum
- Use proceeds to fund **real estate, trusts, or long-term investments**

If you're not planning your exit, you're just running in circles.

And when you're ready to pass the torch:

- Create a **step-by-step guide** for your heirs or partners
- List all credit accounts, banks, passwords, and automation flows

- Ensure your business and credit structures are legally transferable

Legacy = Leverage + Structure + Intention

The Final Move That Changed Marcus's Family Forever

More Than Just a Number

Marcus Tran had hit the number.

After three years of strategic credit building, stacking, vendor relationships, and disciplined business spending, he had **$1.2 million in combined personal and business credit.**

He'd built a successful logistics company and digital trucking academy, and his credit profile was flawless—scores above 780, $300K in revolving business cards, $250K in personal credit limits, and two $250K lines of credit from his banks.

But something felt unfinished.

One night, while reviewing his credit dashboard, he thought:

> "What happens if I'm not here tomorrow? Who knows how to run this? Who can access it? Who owns it?"

That was the moment Marcus shifted from **growth mode to legacy mode.**

From Builder to Architect

Marcus knew how to grow credit. But he hadn't prepared his family to inherit it—or the wealth it enabled.

His wife, a nurse, had no idea how the business cards worked or why one bank reported to Equifax and another to D&B.

His teenage daughter thought "business credit" was just a fancy way to get a car with no cosigner.

So Marcus got serious. He didn't just want to pass on his money—he wanted to pass on the **blueprint.**

He hired an estate planner. Created a **living trust**. Reorganized all credit cards under the business EIN. Transferred digital course ownership into an LLC holding company. Set up a family operating agreement.

Then he made a simple decision: **Every credit line would now fund income-producing assets only.**

No more shiny tools. No new gadgets. Just leverage turned into lasting value.

Turning Credit Into Capital

Marcus mapped out his next year of credit use differently.

He used $25,000 from a 0% Amex to fund:

- Audiobook production
- Facebook ads for a digital trucking mentorship
- A rebrand with a top-tier designer

That led to a **$12,000/month passive funnel** within 60 days.

Then he used $40,000 from his business LOC to:

- Purchase land in a growing city for a trucking lot
- Build a small pre-fab office
- Hire a VA to manage appointments

Six months later, he was leasing the space to a new trucking startup for **$4,000/month**, netting $2,800 after costs.

> "I realized I didn't need a million in cash. I just needed a million in credit I used with purpose."

Teaching the Next Generation

Marcus sat down with his daughter, now a high school senior, and showed her how credit really worked.

Not just how to swipe—but how to apply strategically, track utilization, build business credit, and keep a Paydex score above 80.

They set up her first LLC together. Helped her sell digital resume templates online. Got her a net-30 vendor account. Watched her first $500 come in—and paid it off from a Divvy business card.

> "My goal isn't to leave her a pile of money," he said. "It's to leave her a skill set and a system that will make her unstoppable."

He printed out a 12-page Credit Legacy Binder with all his accounts, passwords, strategies, and structures—just in case.

The Legacy Blueprint

Today, Marcus still runs his businesses—but with a new mission.

His credit is no longer just for growth. It's for **infrastructure.**

- He funds investment property rehabs
- He launches digital products with his kids
- He uses business credit to test ideas without risk

- He holds quarterly "Credit Meetings" with his family, just like profit reviews

And when he mentors other entrepreneurs, he always ends with this:

> "You didn't come this far just to get more cards. You came this far so that one day, someone else can say: I didn't have to start from scratch—because someone left me a path."

Marcus turned $1M in credit into **a permanent financial blueprint**—for himself, his children, and generations to come.

Final Words from the Author: "Credit Is Just the Beginning"

A Journey Most Will Never Take

If you've made it this far, you've already done something most people won't—**you committed to mastering credit, not just using it.**

Most people treat credit like a lifeline. A way to survive until payday. A shortcut to buy something they can't afford.

But you and I—we've chosen a different path.

We've chosen to use credit as a **bridge to something bigger.** Something lasting. Whether that's a business, a property, a family legacy, or just peace of mind—you now know that credit, when used wisely, is **the most powerful financial tool available.**

This book wasn't just about credit cards or scores. It was about **control. Leverage. Ownership. And growth.**

And those don't expire like a promotional APR.

What I Want You to Remember

Here's what I hope stays with you long after you close this audiobook:

- **You don't need money to make money—you need strategy.**
- Your **credit score is a reflection of habits**, not luck.
- Personal credit is the foundation; **business credit is the accelerator.**
- The more you automate, monitor, and separate your systems, the **less risk you carry**.
- Real wealth isn't measured in credit limits—it's measured in what you build with them.

If you can build a business or buy a cash-flowing asset without risking your personal finances... If you can sleep at night knowing your systems are clean and your reports are accurate... Then you're not just managing credit. You're mastering it.

A Note to Builders, Hustlers, and Visionaries

To the builders: If you're grinding right now—building on nights, weekends, or after the kids are in bed—I see you.

Keep going. The habits you're building today will become the systems that protect you tomorrow.

To the hustlers: If you're stacking credit, launching offers, and scaling fast—slow down just enough to stay smart. One mistake can cost you months. One system can save you years.

To the visionaries: If you're thinking big—building for your family, your legacy, your future—start documenting everything. Teach your kids. Create the blueprint.

> You didn't come this far to build something that ends with you.

You came this far to **pass something down**. Something that will live longer than any single account, score, or lender.

What's Next?

This book is part of a larger movement—**Credit to Capital**—because my goal isn't to help you chase credit. My goal is to help you **convert it into real capital, real income, and real assets**.

So what's next for you?

- Build a cash-flowing asset from your first $5K in business credit

- Start teaching others what you've learned
- Get your family involved in credit building
- Establish trusts, LLCs, or legacy plans that separate you from your money
- Or simply review your accounts this week and ask:

  "Am I in control—or just reacting?"

Remember, you can always grow from where you are right now. Even if you're starting with a 580 score and a $300 secured card—you can get to $1M.

> I started with less than that—and so did many of the people in this book.

A Personal Thank You

Thank you for listening.

You could have chosen a hundred other books, podcasts, or distractions—but you chose to invest in your financial growth. That means something.

I didn't write this book to impress you. I wrote it to **equip you.**

I want you to walk away from this with more than just knowledge—I want you to walk away with a new identity.

You're no longer just a borrower. You're no longer just an applicant. You are a **strategic, structured, and respected financial player**.

And if we meet one day, I hope you'll tell me:

> "I didn't just get $1M in credit. I built something that changed my family forever."

Until then, stay disciplined. Stay strategic. And never forget:

Credit is just the beginning. Capital is the key. But what you build with it... that's your legacy.

Joe Correa

Epilogue: "From Credit to Legacy – What Comes After the $1M Milestone"

You're Not the Same Person Anymore

By now, you've gone through dozens of tools, tactics, and true stories. You've built systems. You've seen how others have turned credit into cash flow, and cash flow into freedom.

But here's the truth: **this journey isn't about the credit anymore.**

It's about what kind of person you became in the process:

- Disciplined
- Focused
- Forward-thinking
- Strategic
- Legacy-minded

You're no longer reacting to bills. You're structuring opportunities. You're no longer building credit. You're building *infrastructure.*

Your access to $1M in credit is just the visible result

of invisible habits.

The Three Phases of Wealth Through Credit

Let's reflect on the phases you just walked through:

Phase 1: Build

You built your personal credit, corrected your habits, and formed your business structure.

Phase 2: Stack

You applied strategically, used bureau diversification, and funded growth through smart credit stacking techniques.

Phase 3: Protect and Multiply

You automated your systems, separated personal and business finances, and used credit to buy back your time and launch legacy plays.

> These three phases are now your new cycle. Every time you hit a new level, you revisit them—but faster, smarter, and with more confidence.

What Wealth Built on Credit Looks Like

You may still be using cards and lines of credit, but look at what they've become:

- A **rental property** with cash flow
- A **digital product** that pays you while you sleep
- A **VA team** that frees up your time
- An **LLC structure** that protects your personal assets
- A **trust** or holding company that your children can inherit

This is how credit turns into **capital**, and capital turns into **assets**, and assets turn into **legacy**.

You've moved beyond spending. You've learned to **build value**.

The Next Evolution — Teaching Others

Once you've reached this level, the next evolution is simple: **become the teacher.**

There are thousands—maybe millions—of people stuck in the same place you were before this book:

- In debt
- Confused about credit
- Afraid of banks

- Relying on bad advice

You don't need to be a guru. Just be the guide.

> Teach your kids. Help your partner. Mentor someone in your community. Or document your own journey for others to follow.

In a world where most people never break out of survival mode, **you now have the blueprint.**

Credit in the Next 10 Years

The credit system is changing fast. AI is underwriting faster than humans. Fintech platforms are replacing traditional banks. Data is becoming more predictive—and less forgiving.

But no matter how technology evolves, **the core principles remain the same**:

- Use less than you're given
- Pay early
- Protect your personal score
- Separate business and personal structures
- Turn borrowed money into recurring revenue

Whether you're building in 2025 or 2035, these rules will keep you ahead of the curve—and eligible for opportunities most people will never even see.

> Because in the end, banks lend to people they trust.
> And now, you've become that person.

The Final Invitation

This book may be over, but your journey isn't.

If this is Book 9 in the *Credit to Capital* series, there's more ahead—more strategies, more stories, more systems to build.

> But now, you're not just listening to the story—you're part of it.

The next time you check your credit, apply for a card, structure a deal, or teach someone else what you've learned... remember what this was all about:

- Not getting approved
- Not chasing points
- Not gaming the system

But building something that **lasts**.

You've gone from credit... To control... To capital... To legacy.

Other Books in the *Credit to Capital* Series

By Joe Correa

Unlock the full financial journey with these powerful and practical books in the *Credit to Capital* series. Each volume is designed to help you build, repair, and leverage credit to create wealth, purchase property, and launch businesses—no matter where you're starting from.

- **Book 1: How to Establish Credit in the U.S.**
- **Book 2: Personal Credit Repair Blueprint**
- **Book 3: How to Build Credit Fast Without Debt**
- **Book 4: Business Credit Mastery**
- **Book 5: Credit Card Secrets for Building Wealth & Rewards**
- **Book 6: Credit Card Hacking for Smart Borrowers**
- **Book 7: How to Leverage Business Credit to Fund Real Estate Purchases**
- **Book 8: Business Credit Ecosystem: Build, Stack & Automate Unlimited Funding Without Personal Risk**
- **Book 9: How to Get $1M in Credit and Keep It**
- **Book 10: Credit-Funded Wealth for Families**

www.ingramcontent.com/pod-product-compliance
Lightning Source LLC
LaVergne TN
LVHW022230200926
848481LV00006B/2197